Digital Delights
for Scrapbooking

SIMPLE TECHNIQUES—DYNAMIC RESULTS

Sue Martin

C&T PUBLISHING

Text © 2006 Sue Martin

Artwork © 2006 C&T Publishing, Inc.

Publisher: Amy Marson

Editorial Director: Gailen Runge

Acquisitions Editor: Jan Grigsby

Editor: Stacy Chamness

Copyeditor/Proofreader: Wordfirm, Inc.

Cover Designer: Kristen Yenche

Design Director/Book Designer: Kristen Yenche

Production Assistant: Kirstie L. Pettersen

Photography: C&T Publishing, Inc., unless otherwise noted

Scrapbook page photography by Sue Martin, unless otherwise noted

Front cover photograph: Olga Filatov

Published by C&T Publishing, Inc., P.O. Box 1456, Lafayette, CA 94549

Library of Congress Cataloging-in-Publication Data

Martin, Sue

 Digital delights for scrapbooking : simple techniques--dynamic results /Sue Martin.

p. cm.

 ISBN-13: 978-1-57120-342-7 (paper trade)

 ISBN-10: 1-57120-342-7 (paper trade)

 1. Photographs--Conservation and restoration--Data processing. 2. Photography--Digital techniques. 3. Photograph albums--Data processing. 4. Scrapbooks--Data processing. 5. Digital preservation. I. Title.

 TR465.M3586 2005

 775--dc22

2005022315

Printed in Singapore

10 9 8 7 6 5 4 3 2 1

Contents

Introduction

When I was a little girl, I always loved crafting and designing gifts to give for birthdays, holidays, and special occasions. The recipients would always rave about my creations, which inspired me to create even more. My mother, my sister, and I were always trying out new techniques for just about every crafting fad that came along. As the years flew by we designed and created gifts using cross-stitch, sewing, quilting, embroidery, macramé, mosaic candle jars, tole painting, papier-mâché, plastic jewelry, Christmas ornaments, and finally the most incredible and everlasting craft of scrapbooking.

I've never experienced a craft that has taken off, and had such an emotional impact on both the designer and the fortunate recipient, as scrapbooking has. One of my fondest memories is of the tears of joy expressed by the mother of my first boyfriend when she opened the scrapbook I created for her back in 1999.

If you are old enough to remember the '70s, the popular craft then was macramé, done by tying various knots and incorporating beads. The trend first started with macraméing hanging plant holders out of jute. Then we advanced to belts out of natural fiber. The ultimate was when nylon macramé rope was introduced in a variety of tacky colors. Of course this was the rage, and as Christmas approached, I quickly started making a macramé circular sunburst—complete with matching beads and a low-budget mirror—for each of my friends and family members. The recipients oohed and aahed when they opened their custom-made, color-coordinated gifts.

I had lived with my boyfriend's loving family for two years and had become very close to his family, especially his mother, Mary. Because her house had blue carpeting, I made Mary a powder blue sunburst with royal blue beads, which she proudly hung on her wall. Fast forward some twenty-plus years, and I was thinking about the family that I had come to love but seldom went to visit. I paid them a visit and, much to my chagrin, that mirror was still hanging on the wall—more hideous than ever. The cords that held the mirror had stretched, and the mirror sagged below the bottom edge. The cheap mirror had also tarnished, which made that sunburst the true ugly duckling in Mary's décor.

Appalled, I asked, "Mary, why do you still have that awful-looking thing on your wall?" Her soft reply was, "Because you made it for me." As I now was in the throes of scrapbooking, I had an idea. "Mary," I asked, "If I make you something else, will you promise to take that thing off the wall?" She assured me she would.

Her son, whom I had dated so many years ago, had been tragically killed in a car wreck when he was 29. I still had some old photos of him racing motorcycles, building my Baja Bug, standing beside his brand-new Ford truck, and playing with his dog, Doobie. I created a 4" × 6" album and presented it to Mary about a week later. As she slowly pored over the book, her eyes filled with tears. "In a few years, when you have another craft, are you going to take this away from me too?" she asked.

Of course I would never do that, but her response left me realizing just how precious handmade gifts are, and especially a scrapbook of memories that can never be replaced.

I've put my heart and soul into scrapbooking techniques over the past several years and want to share my enthusiasm, designs, and techniques developed with those of you who share my passion.

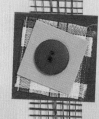

YOU, TOO, CAN TAKE
perfect photos

Great scrapbook pages start with great photos. I've compiled a list of tips that I've used over the years to make my photos shine. Try these techniques yourself when you have time to experiment with your camera. You'll soon be shooting photos like the pros.

Fix the Cool Tones

If you already own a digital camera, you have probably noticed how outdoor photos may tend to have a blue-green cast or cool tone. Most digital cameras have white balance set to "auto," with an option to manually adjust it for different lighting conditions. To determine the white balance, the camera picks a white point in the image and then sets the rest of the color tone to most accurately reflect the white in the photo. Setting the white balance to accurately reflect the present lighting will cause a color shift in the photo.

To correct the oversaturation of green or blue, change the white balance to cloudy, which will increase the reds and yellows to warm up your photo. You can also manually set the white balance. Zoom in on a white spot/section of your subject, set the white balance, and then resume taking your picture. If your subject does not have any white on it, place a white card (preferably not glossy) in the center of the subject and zoom in to set the white balance.

The key to white balance is to set it to match the lighting that the subject is in. When taking a photo in fluorescent lighting, set the white balance to fluorescent; in tungsten lighting set it to tungsten, and so on.

Photo taken with white balance set to 0

Photo taken with white balance set to cloudy

Sunglasses:
The Portable "Polarizers"

A frustration with outdoor photography is the glare and reflections that can be seen on eyeglasses, metallic objects such as cars, and even glistening, suntanned bodies. A great way to reduce glare and unwanted reflections is to use a polarizing filter. Many cameras have a variety of optional filters that can be screwed onto the main lens. If your camera does not allow for adding lens filters, simply use your polarized sunglasses. Place the lens as close as you can to the camera lens, being sure the sunglasses' frame is out of the way of the camera lens. For the best results, make sure that the sun is behind you and at a 90° angle, just over one of your shoulders.

Photo taken without polarizer

 A polarized lens will not only reduce the glare; it will also enhance the photo and make the blue skies bluer and the green plants greener.

Photo taken with polarized sunglasses used as a filter

Perfect Outdoor Photography

The best time to take outdoor photos is just after sunrise or just before sunset when the sunlight is not too intense. But, as many awesome photo opportunities occur right in the middle of the day, you will need to make some minor adjustments to take better photos in bright light.

If you live in a sunny environment, you know how the intense sunlight can overilluminate your subject, making it difficult to take great outdoor shots. You can solve this problem by taking advantage of your camera's flash or fill-flash mode so that you control the flash and turn it on when you need it. When the flash is on, the camera exposes the background first and then adds the right amount of flash to illuminate your subject in the foreground.

Try putting your subject completely under the shade of a tree; then use the flash to illuminate him. This keeps him cool and relaxed, and will prevent him from closing or squinting his eyes. The flash will brighten the subject, helping prevent dark shadows, such as those under the brim of a hat.

Bear in mind that the flash will only work up to ten feet away, so be sure you are close enough to your subject. If you yourself are in the sunshine while taking the photo, hold a card above the camera to shade it from any direct sunlight.

MOUNTAIN MAN

Cardstock: Bazzill Basics

Transparency film

Paint: Delta Ceramcoat

Rub-on letters: Autumn Leaves

Leather, beads, and beadwork from my stash

Fill-Flash

Most cameras include a fill-flash mode, which can help decrease dark shadows. Fill-flash overrides your camera's autoflash mode, causing the flash to fire even in bright light.

Zoom In on the Little Things

As a child, I loved challenging my siblings to find the coolest bug crawling beneath the grass. My brothers loved the earwigs, and the girls' favorites were the roly-poly bugs. It's fun to recollect my childhood discoveries by photographing the little creatures that live among us.

Use your camera's macro mode (often designated by a tulip icon) to zoom in on tiny subjects such as flowers or bees. Get as close to the bee as your camera (and the bee!) will allow (usually about seven to twelve inches), press the shutter down halfway to focus, and then when the confirmation light goes on, press the shutter the rest of the way. This will give you a crisp image of the bee and soften the plant behind it. Be sure to take plenty of photos because these creatures can be hard to capture as they are flitting about. You will probably have several fuzzy photos among the great ones.

When practicing with your macro mode, try taking photos of tiny stationary items such as flowers. This will help you get the feel of focusing on the specific portion of the image that you want to be crisp and will let everything else blur into the background, without you having to worry about chasing the subject, as you would with insects.

tip

Macro Photography
Use close-up photography, where the image is larger than life size, to enhance and show minute details.

Photo of a bee taken in macro mode

Straighten Your Horizons

It tends to be difficult to hold a digital camera level when using the LCD screen as your viewfinder. Oftentimes when you are taking photos of landscapes, monuments, or buildings, the subject will be lopsided or tilted.

The optics in the camera will often distort the image on the LCD screen, so we tend to overcorrect the image by tilting the camera. The best solution is to use a tripod, but that can be awkward to carry around and it certainly won't help with impromptu photos.

An easy solution is to take several shots, intentionally tilting your camera to the left and right as well as shooting straight on. Then, when you view them on a computer screen, save the good one and delete the rest.

Another easy way to straighten a photo is to use your image-editing software. Select the photo, rotate it using the rotation tools, and then crop off the crooked edges. No one will ever know that your original was crooked. They'll simply think you're an awesome photographer!

If your camera has a panorama feature, use it! Panoramic shots make a stunning addition to your layout. It's best to use a tripod to steady the camera, but if one is not available, use something stationary such as a pole or a tabletop to stabilize your camera. Some cameras, such as the HP Photosmart R707, have a built-in panorama mode. After you take the first picture, an outline of an object on the left side of the first photo appears. Use this outline to overlap the next section of the photo. After taking three to five photos, use the in-camera stitching software to stitch the individual photos into one panoramic photo.

There are many easy-to-use software programs, such as ArcSoft Panorama Maker, that can accomplish the same task on your computer.

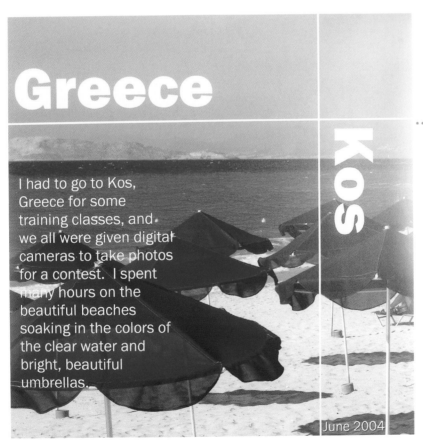

GREECE

HP Creative Scrapbooking Assistant software

HP Premium Plus photo paper

Font: CAC Leslie

Photo rotated and cropped in an image-editing program to straighten the horizon (You can see more of the original photo on the Escape to Kos layout.)

Photo taken with the camera on a tripod

PARADISE FOUND

Background paper: Dolphin Enterprises

Rub-on letters: Autumn Leaves

Simply Stated rub-on transfers: Making Memories

Teri Martin sticker: Creative Imaginations

HP Creative Scrapbooking Assistant software

ESCAPE TO KOS

Cardstock: Bazzill Basics

Paper: Carol Wilson Fine Arts

Fibers: EK Success Adornments

Brads, Simply Stated rub-on transfers:
    Making Memories

Sonnets Poemstones by Sharon Soneff:
    Creative Imaginations

Tag from my stash

Font: Scriptina

Panoramic photo taken with a 5.1 MP camera (HP Photosmart R707)

Picture Perfect 8 × 10s

Although called by different names on different cameras, most digital cameras have "normal," "better," and "best" modes. The "best" mode will be the highest-resolution mode. Always use this mode when shooting your photos. While a low resolution allows you to store more photos on your card, the higher resolution guarantees that you can always enlarge an excellent photo to an 8″ × 10″ or even to a full-size 12″ × 12″ layout.

The highest resolution is also great for taking long-distance shots, such as at a soccer game. Be sure to use only the optical zoom for these faraway shots. The digital zoom simply crops the image in the camera, and you lose some quality. When you save the photo to your computer, you can crop and enlarge it without losing any quality.

PHOTO SIZE	PIXEL COUNT AT 300 DPI
4″ × 6″	1200 × 1800
5″ × 7″	1500 × 2100
8″ × 10″	2400 × 3000
12″ × 14″	3600 × 4200

The megapixel rating in your camera also determines how large a high-quality print can be. The table to the right shows the print sizes that can be generated from cameras with the following megapixel ranges:

MEGAPIXELS IN CAMERA	LARGEST HIGH-RESOLUTION PRINTS
1 to 1.9	3″ × 5″
2 to 2.9	5″ × 7″
3 to 3.9	8″ × 10″
4 to 5	12″ × 12″
6 +	13″ × 19″

 Resolution

Image resolution describes how much image detail an image contains. The higher the resolution, the more image detail in a photo, and the larger the file size. High resolution means clearer photos that can be printed larger; usually expressed in dots per inch, or DPI, a 300 DPI photo is considered high resolution.

Photo taken with a 4.0 MP camera (HP 850) in "best" mode

MAGICAL MEMORIES

Patterned paper: The Robin's Nest

Fibers: EK Success Adornaments

Tags, mesh, clips, stars: Making Memories

Alphadotz, conchos: Scrapworks

Wire: Artistic Wire

Photo taken with a 5.1 MP camera (HP R707) in "best" mode

SEASIDE

Cardstock: Bazzill Basics

Fibers: EK Success Adornments,
   Making Memories Funky with Fibers

Slide mounts, Seaside vellum: Magic Scraps

Shaker box: Paper Bliss

Embossing powder: PSX

Transparency film

Sand, sand dollar, brads from my stash

Pixels and Megapixels

Tiny dots make up a picture in a computer. Each of these dots is called a pixel. A megapixel is 1 million pixels. Cameras with more megapixels contain less information in each pixel, creating a clearer photograph that can be printed larger.

WHEN THE SUN GOES DOWN

Clip art: Cottagearts.net

HP Creative Scrapbook Assistant software

HP Premium Plus Photo Paper

Font: Papyrus

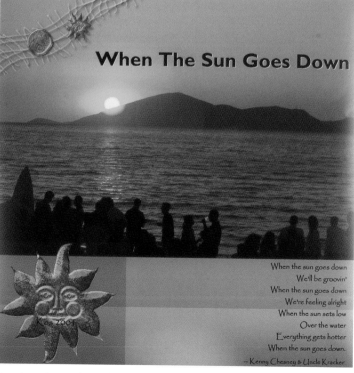

Another photo taken with a 5.1 MP camera (HP R707) in "best" mode

Steady as She Goes

A tripod ensures that your photos won't be out of focus due to shaky hands. Yes, it can be bulky and a pain to cart around, but there are small, lightweight tripods available that can fit in your purse or back pocket. You can find a whole assortment of mini tripods from four to nine inches tall at www.minitripods.com. Another handy item to keep with your camera supplies is a small beanbag. It can be set on a boulder or on a tree branch and the camera can rest on it to take a steady shot.

A tripod is also very useful if you want to be in the picture as well. My boys have complained on several occasions that there are very few pictures of me in their albums, because I'm typically the photographer. Now I use a tripod so that I am in many of the photos.

Use the self-timer and make sure that the focusing sensor is pointed at one person in the group, not the background. Otherwise you'll have fuzzy people and a very sharp and detailed background.

Denny's favorite sport is golf and he goes out as often as possible. We always take him golfing as a family for Father's Day. Lawrence Welk's Fountains course is perfect for all of us — not too long for Sue, Tyler, and Kyle.

June 2003

DAD

Aqua gingham paper: K&Company

Cardstock: Bazzill Basics

Aquamarine vellum: EK Success—Over the Moon Press

Watercolor vellum from my stash

Embossing powder: PSX

"DAD" embellishments: Meri Meri (I modified the "A" with the yellow background and golf flag)

Golf flag sticker: Jolee's Boutique

Pewter oval: Making Memories

Fibers: knitting scraps from my mother

Eyelets from my stash

tip

Note

Throughout the book I have listed sources and/or companies where embellishments have come from, but occasionally I am unable to recollect where I bought a certain item. In these instances, I've noted that the item is simply "from my stash."

It was so fun to have Marcia visit for a mini family reunion. Sandra, Kirk, Scott, and Vienna all came over for lunch. Marcia hadn't seen Sara since she was a baby and Adam was only two.

Marcia's Visit

Family photo taken with a tripod to include Mom

MARCIA'S VISIT

Cardstock: Bazzill Basics

Tracy Porter Floral Tapestry Paper: ColorBök

Green paper: Paper Adventures

Plaid paper, vellum, buttons from my stash

Rub-on alphabet: Making Memories

Flower brads: Queen & Company

intriguing photos

Photo Paper

With the right photo paper, digital photos will last longer than traditional photos. No matter what brand of photo printer you have, always use photo paper manufactured by your printer vendor. Each vendor has chemists who formulate the inks and paper to work best together. If you use another vendor's paper, you are likely to get poor results. There are literally hundreds of types of papers on the market, and each one will create a different look.

High-quality photo paper is a must to guarantee that your photos will look professional and will endure over time. With inkjet photos, the concern about longevity is based on exposure to light. Photos will start fading after a certain period of time if they are exposed to too much light. Our scrapbooks, for the most part, are closed and on a shelf until we share them, so there is not such a concern with photos in our albums fading.

Different paper and ink combinations will vary drastically in terms of the length of time the photo will be crisp and clear. For example, Hewlett-Packard has HP Premium Plus photo paper that, when used with its six-ink, eight-ink, and nine-ink printers, will not show signs of fading for over 100 years. Other vendors may make similar claims, so be sure to consult with the experts before purchasing photo paper for your printer. Check out the Wilhelm Imaging Research website for up-to-date information on photo longevity with all photo printers (www.wilhelm-research.com).

 To prevent your photos from sticking to the page protector (or each other), use a matte-finish paper and let them dry for 24 hours.

Photo by Olga Filatov

Printed on HP Premium Plus photo paper with an HP Photosmart 8450 photo printer

Printed on Epson photo paper with an HP Photosmart 8450 photo printer

Printed on Canon photo paper on an HP Photosmart 8450 photo printer

Special Effects Printing

There are many software programs that allow you to edit your digital images. Two of the more popular ones are Adobe Photoshop and Adobe Photoshop Elements (trial versions can be downloaded from the Adobe website; see Sources, page 62). Some of the effects that you can apply are color variations such as black and white, sepia, and antique; artistic effects such as watercolor; and negatives.

I use my HP Photosmart printers to convert my photos to black and white, sepia, or antique directly from the camera memory cards, without using a computer.

The following series of layouts shows how changing the color of the photo can affect the entire mood and feeling of the design.

Photo by Olga Filatov

A LITTLE MIRACLE

Cardstock: Bazzill Basics

Patterned paper: The Paper Loft

Vellum: Scrapbook Sally

Large bookplate frame: Li'l Davis Designs

Brads, phrases: Making Memories

Printed on photo paper

Photo by Olga Filatov

ANASTASIA

Cardstock: Bazzill Basics

Pink Watercolor paper: Memory Bound

Scrapper's Canvas, rub-on letters:
    Creative Imaginations

Simple Sayings sticker: Bo-Bunny Press

Baby rickrack: Wrights

Printed on canvas. Notice how the baby's complexion is smoothed out and looks hand painted.

Printed in sepia on photo paper

LAUGH

Cardstock: Bazzill Basics

Patterned paper: Autumn Leaves—Rhonna Farrer

CHERISH

Cardstock: Bazzill Basics

Patterned paper, tag: BasicGrey

Distress ink: Ranger Industries

Ribbon: Michaels stores

Cherish sticker: Déjà Views

Printed in antique on photo paper

OUR BUNDLE OF JOY

Cardstock: Bazzill Basics

Floral tapestry paper: Tracy Porter—Colorbök

Bundle of Joy embellishment: Li'l Davis Designs

Embossing ink: Versamark

Ultra-Thick Embossing Enamel: Suze Weinberg

Embossing powder: PSX

Fibers: EK Success Adornments

Brads: Making Memories

Font: Lucida Handwriting

Photo by Olga Filatov

Our Darling Anastasia,

When they say a picture is worth a thousand words, they must have had you in mind. Your joyous smile emanates from within and brightens the day of all who witness it. I've had people stop me in the grocery store to admire you and tell me what a beauty you are. My only wish for you is that your physical beauty is permeated into your emotional beauty. I have no doubt that you will grow into a beautiful child, teen, and adult, that shows the world that the younger generation can and will make a difference.

All my love...Mom

our bundle of joy

Printed in black and white on photo paper

Black and White

Black-and-white photos really allow you to expand your color palette of background pages and embellishments. In black and white, your photos do not compete with the colors on the page. It's very easy to convert a digital photo to black and white by simply changing the setting in your printer driver from color printing to black and white (sometimes indicated as *grayscale*). This will not affect your original photo but will simply convert it to black and white before printing it.

Photo scanned in and converted to black and white to remove yellow ageing, then printed on canvas

SENSITIVE

Cardstock: Bazzill Basics

Scrapper's Canvas: Creative Imaginations

Embossing powder: PSX

Vellum from my stash

HP Creative Scrapbook Assistant software

Fonts: Rockwell, Times New Roman,
    Goudy Old Style, Bickley Script, Book Antiqua

MEN IN BLACK

Paper: Memories Complete, Mustard Moon

Vellum, white mesh: Colorbök

Black mesh: Maruyama Magenta

Photo corners, dots, scrolls, metal mesh,
    washers: Making Memories

Ribbons: Michaels stores

Font: Pepita MT

Sepia

Sepia photos were very popular back in the '60s and '70s. With their monochromatic brown tones, they work well with busy patterned papers because they don't compete with the color schemes. You can stay with neutral earth tones or bring in a color such as a smoky blue for highlights. I converted these color photos to sepia by using the color options in my HP Photosmart 8450 printer.

AUTHOR, AUTHOR

Paper: Autumn Leaves

Brad bars: Karen Foster Design

Paint: Plaid

Fresh verse vellum: Déjà Views

Vellum from my stash

Fonts: Vintage Typewriter, Stencil, Verdana, Rockwell Extra Bold

MISSING BEN

HP Creative Scrapbook Assistant software

Font: Tahoma

 If your printer or your image-editing software does not have a sepia option, you can create the results yourself in four easy steps. The example shown is in Photoshop Elements.

1. **Choose Image > Mode > RGB color**
2. **To discard color information, choose Enhance > Adjust color > Remove color**
3. **Choose Enhance > Adjust color > Color Variations, and select Midtones in the Color Variations box**
4. **Choose Decrease red, and Increase blue (they have pre-set amounts)**

Antique

"Antique" photos work extremely well with heritage and shabby chic pages. The subdued pastels truly put you back in time so that you feel like you were there. They can also produce a calming look on a potentially busy page. I created the antique photo below by converting the color photo with my HP Photosmart 8450 printer.

Kyle,

One of my *fondest* [   ] of your childhood was helping you achieve your [   ] of becoming an *Eagle Scout*. Your [   ] has been both challenging and exciting. [   ] in yourself and the future will **reward** you with the Boy Scouts highest honor. Always [   ] your scouting [   ] and how they [   ] you to "**do your best**". You are an **awesome** kid with awesome potential.

Love you always,

LETTER TO KYLE

Cardstock: Bazzill Basics

Paper, sheet metal: Scrap-Ease

Mesh: Magic Mesh

Bugs, leaves: Paper Bliss

Tea-dyed muslin: Daisy D's

Leaf stickers: Stickopotamus

BE PREPARED

Cardstock: Bazzill Basics

Borders, journal box, tags: Paper Bliss

Scout oath and motto: It Takes Two

Transparency film

Paper, jute from my stash

Font: CK Journaling

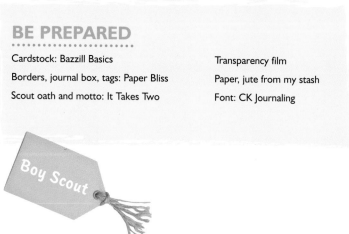

tip You can also accomplish this in image-editing software by adjusting the image and lowering the saturation by 70%. In Photoshop Elements it's done in two easy steps; most photo-editing programs will have comparable steps.

1. Choose Enhance > Adjust Color > Adjust Hue/Saturation
2. Type in -70 in the Saturation box to reduce the saturation by 70%

Photo Collages

Have you ever had many great photos of one event and wanted to include them all in your layout? Photo collages are a fun and easy way to add several photos on one page. I use this technique when I have a lot of great pictures of a single event, such as a birthday party, and I only want to do a one- to two-page spread. The entire collage can then be matted and added to the page along with a title, journaling, and embellishments. When creating a collage, it's also fun to leave one of the photo spots empty so that an embellishment can be added as an accent.

There are numerous software programs that offer a variety of photo collage templates. The examples I've shown use the collage templates in the HP photo imaging software that came with the HP Photosmart 7960 photo printer.

'TIS THE SEASON

Plaid paper: Paper Pizazz

Dreamy Dots willow paper: Making Memories

Green paper with gold leaves from my stash

Cardstock: Bazzill Basics

Christmas tree-shaped journalette: Creating Keepsakes

Clip art: Creating Keepsakes

Star-shaped brads: Creative Imaginations

Metallic thread: Kreinik

Wire: Artistic Wire

Seed and bugle beads from my stash

Fonts: Broadway, CK Journaling, CK Diva

tip

Journaling

Write your thoughts and details of the photos or event on your page layout.

SPRING TIME

Cardstock: Colorbök

Royal Tapestry, Paradise plaid
  papers: Karen Foster Design

Vellum: Autumn Leaves

Brads: Lost Art Treasures

Clip art: Creating Keepsakes

Slide mounts from my stash

Font: CK Journaling

KING OF THE GRILL

Cardstock: Bazzill Basics

Cooking accessory embellishments:
  Jolee's Boutique

Wire: Artistic Wire

Maine-shaped journalette:
  Creating Keepsakes

Paper, vellum, beads from my stash

Font: CK Journaling

I've never seen the boys with such endless grins and smiles. Our vacation to Orlando was awesome! We stayed at the Coronado Springs Resort and it was as much fun as some of the theme parks. Every day, the boys and I went to the pool. It was huge and even had a long, twisting water slide. Kyle loved climbing up the pyramid. We also rented the four seater bikes and rode all around the hotel.

p u r e

e c s t a s y

joy

laugh

love

PURE ECSTASY

Funky Bubbles and Water Speckle papers, transparencies: NRN Designs

Blue Jean, Swimming Pool, Mega Plaid papers: Doodlebug Design

Icy Textures paper: Karen Foster Design

Sonnets Poemstones by Sharon Soneff: Creative Imaginations

Decorative chalk: Craf-T Products

Font: CK Journaling

Photo Matting

When I have a photo that is truly outstanding, I love to print it out twice, trim the edges ⅛″ all the way around, and then pop-dot the smaller photo on top of the larger one. This 3-D effect can really enhance the photo.

Mat Your Photos

Use acid-free adhesive or photo tabs to stick a photo on the paper you want to mat with. Trim around the photo, leaving as wide (or narrow) a border as you desire.

Another technique I use is to punch a portion of the photo with a square punch, and pop-dot the punched photo on top of the full-size photo.

Pop-Dot

Use this technique to pop up a photo or embellishment for a 3-D effect. With two-sided tape, stick a photo (or any artwork you'd like to feature) on a small piece of foam, then stick the foam to the page.

Printing a second photo in a reduced size is a lovely way to mat your journal box. In the Gardening layout below, I printed a 2″ × 3″ photo of the lantana flowers, then printed journaling on vellum and added it to the photo. It really helps tie all the components together. With *Winter Blossom* I went a step further and double-matted the photo. The bottom layer is printed on Fredrix Tygerag, which is similar to a Tyvek envelope except that it has been treated to accept ink. After I printed the photo, I heated the Tygerag with a heat gun, which slightly melted, shrunk, and buckled the photo. I then placed an ironing cloth over the Tygerag and ironed it to make it flat. The final step was to sew the Tygerag to my background paper and add the photos on top.

GARDENING

Cardstock: Bazzill Basics

Backyard, Finishing Touches cardstocks:
    Cloud Nine Design

Mango yarn: Lion Brand

Fibers: Four Sisters Creations

Embossing powder: PSX

Vellum from my stash

There is nothing more beautiful than a winter blossom. This bromeliad brightens up our dreary front porch in February.

WINTER BLOSSOM

Striped paper: Colorbök

Green paper: Mrs. Grossman's

Tygerag: Fredrix

Bobbin ribbon: Michaels stores

Fonts: Scriptina, Tahoma

Journal Box

Journal your thoughts on a piece of paper and cut it into a shape. It doesn't have to be a square or rectangle—it could be a heart, a leaf, a star, or . . .

Masking

Masking is a technique in which you use die-cut letters or hand-cut shapes and temporarily adhere them to a sheet of vellum or transparency film prior to printing the photo, using a temporary adhesive such as Hermafix (by EK Success: see Sources, page 62). After the photo is printed you remove the letters and the clear space will allow your background paper to show through. The letters you remove can then be used again on the same layout, or you can use them on a complementary page. This effect can also be achieved digitally by typing white letters on the photo in a photo-editing program. Because printers can't print white ink, nothing will be printed where the letters are, leaving clear words.

1. Print the photo on a plain piece of paper.

3. Carefully apply a temporary adhesive to the back of each letter. Press the letters onto the printable side of the transparency film and smooth all edges.

2. Place the die cuts on the photo to see where you want them to appear on the final photo.

4. Print the photo and then remove the letters. Attach the photo to a colored or printed background page.

ROWING

Cardstock: Bazzill Basics

Paint: Delta Ceramcoat
(I mixed the colors myself.)

Brads: Making Memories

Transparency film

Fonts: Century, CAC Camelot,
CAC Crazy Legs, Arial

Kyle earned his twelfth merit badge at Camp Emerald Bay. Rowing was a challenge and frustrating at first, but he had a blast as soon as he mastered it.

Created digitally by typing white letters on the photo then printing on transparency film

When we went to Vegas for Kyle's 13th birthday, Tyler was the big winner and won Lizzy by tossing a wooden ring onto a wine bottle. Lizzy quickly became the family mascot, and we couldn't wait to take photos of all the kids and grandkids. Tyler, Kyle, Adam, Sara, Chase and Alicia, were the perfect models.

LIZZY

Paper: K&Company, Creative Memories

Cardstock: Bazzill Basics

Paint: Plaid

Metal word plate: American Crafts

Fibers: EK Success Adornments, Making
Memories Funky with Fibers

Family tag: Creative Imaginations

Alphabet stamps from my stash

Fonts: Verdana, Kristen ITC, Brush Script ITC,
Snap ITC, Lucida Handwriting

There are so many wonderful types of paper, fabric, and vellum that will really enhance your scrapbooks and make them unique. I love experimenting with everything, and I love to see how photos and journaling will look when printed on the variety of media that's available. Some materials prove to be more difficult to send through a printer because of the way the paper feeds through it. The straight paper path (when the paper does not turn inside the machine) offers the greatest flexibility, but many different papers and vellums will print well in most printers if you prepare them properly. The more you practice, the better you will understand the capabilities of your printer. Have fun with your printer. It's a fabulous scrap tool!

Printable Fabric

Using printable fabric is a fun and elegant way to print photos and embellishments. Printable fabric typically comes in white and ivory/cream, and each color has its benefits in terms of adding luxury to a page. Printable fabric has a paper backing that is adhered with temporary adhesive so it will feed well through your printer. After the sheet is printed, simply peel off the backing and you're ready to crop and add your photo or title to your scrapbook page.

When printing photos, I typically use white fabric for color and black-and-white photos, and ivory for sepia and antique-colored photos.

For an aged or shabby look, try fraying the edges after printing. Pull one thread from the top of the photo from left to right to remove it. Continue removing as many threads as you like on both the horizontal and vertical edges. A complementary title or journal box that is also frayed is a nice way to finish your page. Fabric can also be easily distressed by lightly sanding the edges with sandpaper.

With a bit of caution, you can also print on twill tape and ribbon. The key to success is using a very sticky double-sided tape to attach the tape or ribbon to a piece of paper before putting it into the printer.

1. Create a line of text in your favorite word-processing program. Print out the text you'll be using on a test piece of copy paper.

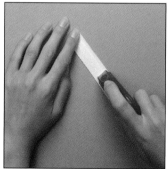

2. Cut a piece of twill tape the length you need. Attach two-sided tape to the back of the twill tape along all edges.

3. Align and adhere the twill tape directly over the printed text on the copy paper. Rub your thumb over the entire piece of twill to secure all edges.

4. Reinsert the page into the printer and print the text again. The text will print directly on the twill tape.

I also like to make my own printable fabric so that I can use different colors and prints. By treating 100% cotton or silk with Bubble Jet Set 2000 (found at fabric stores or on the Internet) and then ironing it to freezer paper, the fabric can be fed through the printer.

HIPPOCRATES

Cardstock: Bazzill Basics

Ivory printable fabric: June Tailor

Walter Knabe Voyage paper,
    harmony stickers: Paper Adventures

Sticko, Architecture stone,
    Nostalgiques metal stencil, stamp,
    tea-stained tag, adhesive tags, type
    sticker alphabets: EK Success

Vellum and fibers from my stash

Font: Papyrus

The photo was printed in both full color and antique modes on fabric to give the feeling of how the columns looked when they were built versus how the ruins look today.

MY WISH FOR YOU

Cardstock: Bazzill Basics

Printable fabric: June Tailor

Metal letters, ribbon charms, eyelet phrases:
    Making Memories

Ribbon: The Card Connection

Decorating chalk: Craf-T Products

Mulberry paper from my stash

Font: Papyrus

The photo was converted to antique and printed on fabric. The journaling scroll was also printed on fabric and hand colored with chalk to complement the page.

BOY S-M-L

Cardstock: Bazzill Basics

Printable fabric: June Tailor

Tags: Junkitz

Square punch: Creative Memories

Embroidery floss: J. & P. Coats

Fibers: Making Memories Funky with Fibers

Buttons from my stash

Font: Verdana

Kyle, you have been the happiest 2-year-old that I've known. Your deep belly-laughs and sparkling blue eyes keep everyone around you smiling. On this visit to the Wild Animal Park, you had so much fun feeding and chasing the ducks. You got especially excited when they would fly and land in the water with a splash.

kyle

The journaling was printed on fabric to complement the fabric accents.

OUR FAMILY

Paper: Provo Craft

Cardstock: Bazzill Basics

Eyelet, quotes, pewter oval book plate: Making Memories

Printable fabric: June Tailor

our family   1998   our family   our family   our family

The title strip was printed on fabric, then cut and frayed.

The title was printed on twill tape.

RENDEZVOUS

Paper: Carolee's Creations

Twill tape: Creative Impressions

Cut-and-tear quotes: Karen Foster Design

Paint: Plaid

Letter "d", Sonnets Poemstones by
Sharon Soneff: Creative Imaginations

Bookplate frame: Li'l Davis Designs

Font: Vintage Typewriter

 On fabric, print photos that are 5″ × 7″ or larger. Smaller prints tend to lose the detail in the grain of the fabric. Change your paper type to "plain" and the print quality to "best."

Printable Canvas

Printable canvas allows you to print fabulous photos that look very professional, yet are inexpensive. The texture is heavier and more prominent than that of printable fabric, so your best results will be on larger prints such as 5″ x 7″, 6″ x 8″, or 8″ x 10″ because you won't lose the detail in the weave. Canvas will also tend to smooth out skin or flaws from an old or poor-quality photo. Look at the series of converted photos on page 16 to see how the baby's skin tone was smoothed to look like it was hand painted when it was printed on canvas in Anastasia. Another example is Sensitive on page 19; the poor-quality photo of my father-in-law was redeemed when enlarged and printed on canvas.

I've found printable canvas in both white and ivory and love them both. Again, I use the ivory for my vintage looks such as sepia and antique, and the white for my color and black-and-white photos.

Photo by Olga Filatov

Babies are Angels that fly to the earth,
Their wings disappear at the time of their birth
One look in their eyes and we're never the same
They're part of us now and that part has a name
That part is your heart and a bond that won't sever
Our Babies are Angels,
We love them forever.
— Unknown

Angel baby

ANGEL BABY

Cardstock: O'Scrap

Scrapper's Canvas: Creative Imaginations

Lipstick Graffiti paper: KI Memories

Simply Stated rub-on transfers, safety pins: Making Memories

Flowers: The Card Connection

Pearls: Magic Scraps

Embossing powder: PSX

Straight 'N' Narrow ribbon: Michaels stores

Vellum from my stash

Font: CK Bella

MEMORIES *of a lifetime*

Nelson and Lorraine Martin were married on August 14, 1939, in Fort Fairfield, Maine. Father Haggarty was the officiating priest at the St. Dennis church. Their reception was held at Sacred Heart Leon Vrmet Hall, which was one half mile away. They honeymooned in Waterville.

August 14

1939

MEMORIES OF A LIFETIME

Cardstock: Bazzill Basics

Scrapper's Canvas: Creative Imaginations

Rub-on letters: Autumn Leaves

HP Creative Scrapbook Assistant software

Ribbon: Michaels stores

Fonts: Times New Roman, Broadway

tip I've found that Glue Dots, 3L tape runner, and Kokuyo tape runner work best for adhering canvas to a page. I've found these in local scrapbook and craft stores, and online.

LOVE AT FIRST SIGHT

Cardstock: Bazzill Basics

Scrapper's Canvas: Creative Imaginations

Rose Damask, Dark Sage paper, Simply Stated rub-on transfers: Making Memories

Lace embellishments: The Venice Lace Collection—Carolace

Loop braid: Wrights

Photo by Olga Filatov

love *at first sight*

The photo was converted to black and white.

Embossing Inkjet Paper

This specialty paper is so much fun! I use it for titles, photos, and journaling. It's a coated paper that allows the ink to stay wet longer, so you have time to sprinkle embossing powder and set it with a heat gun. Bright-colored fonts seem to jump off the page when printed on this paper. Photos of water, such as lakes and beach scenes, come to life when printed and embossed. Also, photos taken in the rain or of children playing in sprinklers are ideal for printing and embossing. Apply Versamark ink and embossing powder to embellishments to make them glisten and complement the photo.

I have not found this paper in scrapbooking stores yet, but it is available on the Web at www.paper-paper.com.

Refer to page 59 for complete embossing instructions.

ALL WET

Striped paper, eyelet letters, details clips:
  Making Memories

Black Mickey paper: Sandylion

Button Ups: Stickopotamus

Versamark embossing ink: Tsukineko

Embossing powder: PSX

Embossing inkjet paper: Micro Format
  Imagination Gallery

Transparency film

Font: CK Man's Print

ADAM IS 5!

Cardstock: Bazzill Basics

Ultra Trim buttons, Double Dipped Coastline, blue paper,
    yellow small dots paper, Funky with Fibers: Making Memories

Blue speckled paper from my stash

Decorating chalk: Craf-T Products

Versamark embossing ink: Tsukineko

Embossing powder: PSX

Embossing inkjet paper: Micro Format Imagination Gallery

WordArt: Microsoft

Transparency Film

Transparency film is a clear plastic sheet that, when treated for inkjet printers, you can print on. Because it is transparent, you can see light through it, so it gives a translucent image. Printing on inkjet transparency film is a clever way to add text, clip art, or photos to things that you can't print on—such as metal, foil, wood, dominoes, glass, pre-printed slick transparency film, tags, and 12″ x 12″ paper if you don't have a large-format printer. I recommend planning a few scrapbook pages with transparency journaling, photos, and titles, then placing each of these items into one document with a computer program such as Microsoft Word or PowerPoint. By doing this you will use as much of the transparency as possible without much waste. Transparency film can be adhered to your page or embellishment using vellum tape, clear glue, brads, eyelets, or stitching.

From **SAND** crab

Adam was **less than thrilled** with his first trip to the beach. The water **scared** him and he **hated** the sand sticking to his feet. He didn't even like sitting on the boogie board. I think it was too close to the **yucky** water and sand. He cried and begged to be picked up. It wasn't until he was safely sitting in a beach chair that his **charming** and **smiling** personality returned.

July 1998

to happy as a **CLAM**

FROM SAND CRAB TO HAPPY AS A CLAM

Paper: Colorbök

Cardstock: Bazzill Basics

Starfish and shells: Dress It Up

David Walker Basic ABC, brads:
    Creative Imaginations

Fun Fur: Lion Brand

Fibers: EK Success Adornaments

Beach shaker box, seashells: Jolee's Boutique

Tags: Paper Bliss

Decorating chalks: Craf-T Products

Eyelets from my stash

Embossing powder: PSX

Transparency film

Fonts: CK Funkie Fun, CK Fill In, CK Anything
    Goes, CK Broad Pen, CK Kiddo, Arial Unicode,
    Britannica Bold, Broadway, Cooper Black,
    Elephant

Transparency Film

There are many different types and brands of transparency film. Be sure to use one appropriate for your printer. I found that Staples even carries a Staples brand transparency film made especially for my Hewlett-Packard inkjet printer!

I **love** this picture of *Kyle* on his 2nd birthday. He always had a **car** in one hand, and even when he got his new *trike*, he wouldn't let go of it. *Grandma JoAnn* got a real kick out of his excitement. Kyle was a huge *Pooh* fan, so his new bear from Aunt Sandra was a hit.

BIRTHDAY BOY

Cardstock: Bazzill Basics

Little Boy Blue splatter paper, simple sayings sticker: Bo-Bunny Press

Wordz, Sonnets Poemstones by Sharon Soneff: Creative Imaginations

Details frames, brads: Making Memories

Fibers: EK Success Adornaments, Making Memories Funky with Fibers

Alphadotz Letters, Hugz frames: Scrapworks

Vellum: American Crafts

Eyelets: JewelCraft

Embossing powder: PSX

Transparency film

Font: Bradley Hand ITC

tip **If you accidentally print on the wrong side of the transparency film, simply wash the ink off with water, dry the film, and try again.**

One of my favorite uses of transparency film is to create the window in a shaker box or photo slide. Traditionally, when you buy shaker box kits the window is completely clear, so you can see all the contents. I like to print a title or phrase on transparency film then cut it out to fit the shaker box, which gives it more depth. I often emboss the ink as well to make it more prominent. (Please refer to page 59 for complete embossing instructions.)

Use your favorite word processor, font, or graphics program to create the text or image that you want to print. Turn on the rulers (found under the Tools tab) so that you can create a perfect fit. Print a test page on plain paper to be sure the size and placement are what you want. Then insert transparency film into the paper tray. There is a right and a wrong side of the transparency film to print on, so read your printer's manual to ensure that you are printing on the correct side. Printing on the wrong side will cause severe smearing, and the ink will not dry.

Mom and Dad were so surprised to see that Sandra wore Mom's wedding dress. Dad didn't even recognize it at first

December, 1984

REMINISCE

Scrapbook Symmetry paper—Twilight: Mrs. Grossman's

Cardstock: Bazzill Basics

Simply Stated rub-on transfers: Making Memories

Paper al Fresco: Paper Adventures

Button Ups: Stickopotamus

Fibers: EK Success Adornaments

Transparency film

Embossing powder: PSX

Embossed navy paper, heart clips from my stash

Font: Angelina

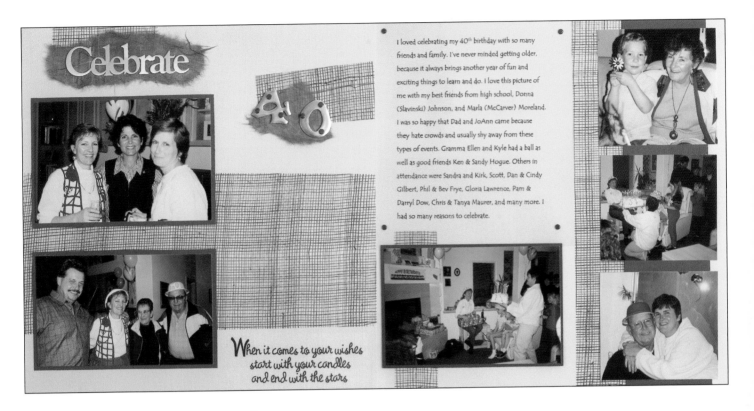

Celebrate

I loved celebrating my 40th birthday with so many friends and family. I've never minded getting older, because it always brings another year of fun and exciting things to learn and do. I love this picture of me with my best friends from high school, Donna (Slavinski) Johnson, and Marla (McCarver) Moreland. I was so happy that Dad and JoAnn came because they hate crowds and usually shy away from these types of events. Gramma Ellen and Kyle had a ball as well as good friends Ken & Sandy Hogue. Others in attendance were Sandra and Kirk, Scott, Dan & Cindy Gilbert, Phil & Bev Frye, Gloria Lawrence, Pam & Darryl Dow, Chris & Tanya Maurer, and many more. I had so many reasons to celebrate.

When it comes to your wishes start with your candles and end with the stars

CELEBRATE 40

Cardstock: Bazzill Basics

Scrap metal "40": Pressed Petals

Mesh: Maruyama Magenta

Simple Sayings: Bo-Bunny Press

Embossing powder: PSX

Transparency film

Mulberry paper and brads from my stash

Font: Tempus Sans ITC

BEACH BABE

Stain collection, twine plaid papers: Making Memories

Denim splatter paper: Bo-Bunny Press

Tokens: Doodlebug Design

Fibers: Making Memories Funky with Fibers

Slide sentiments: Magic Scraps

Pthalo Blue and white paints: Delta Ceramcoat

Clip art: CK Lettering

Embroidery floss: J. & P. Coats

Label Lingo: EK Success

Transparency film

50 IS FIVE PERFECT 10'S

Cardstock: Bazzill Basics

Numbers, frames: Scrapworks

Simple Sayings: Bo-Bunny Press

Chunky Layover: Making Memories

Danelle Johnson Sophisticate alphabet stickers; Shotz Basic ABCs, Scrapbook Stickerz—David Walker; Sonnets Poemstones by Sharon Soneff: Creative Imaginations

Curly Alphabet stickers: Me & My Big Ideas

Embossing powder: PSX

Transparency film

Font: Verdana

The journaling is hidden behind one of the group shots.

VIVA MEXICO

Cardstock: Bazzill Basics

Paint: Delta Ceramcoat

Ribbon words: Making Memories

Mesh: Maruyama Magenta

Hinges: The Card Connection

Transparency film

Sombrero die cut, oval word, frame, brads, and woven
bracelets from my stash

Font: Tahoma

helping AUntie sUe

Adam had so much fun pulling all of the videos out of the cabinet. It just seemed like the right thing to do. It's an **Aunt's** prerogative to let her **adorable nephew** enjoy his video scattering.
April 1994

should you need
a
helping hand,
i'll gladly lend you
mine.

HELPING AUNTIE SUE

Simple Sets Soapstone paper: S.E.I.

Alphawordz, Alphadotz letters, Hugz frames: Scrapworks

Friendship vellum: Memories Complete

Embossing powder: PSX

Transparency film

Font: Verdana

tip Change your printer to transparency mode (found in the Properties menu— see your printer's user guide for details), which will apply less ink to the page. Heat embossing will permanently set the ink so it will never smear. (See page 59 for embossing instructions.)

Vellum

The vellum that we buy in scrapbooking stores is actually a coated paper. Most types will work well with your inkjet printer. I love layering with vellum, and it is a wonderful medium for printing titles and journal boxes. It's also a great way to print a photo that you overlay on textured paper, such as in Kos at Dusk below. Notice how the silver stars are softly illuminated in the darkening sky.

Soft or pastel colors work best when creating a journal box. Patterned vellums can also be used as long as the pattern is not too busy.

KOS AT DUSK

Beaded star paper and vellum from my stash

Mesh: Magic Mesh

Alphabet charms: Making Memories

Font: Papyrus

 If your only photo of a special memory is of poor quality, try printing it on vellum to help smooth out the flaws.

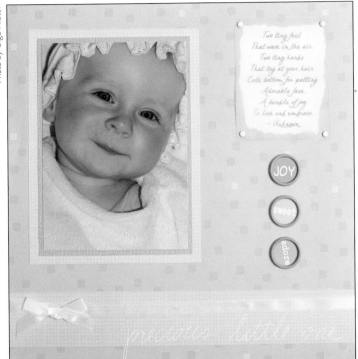

Two tiny feet
That wave in the air
Two tiny hands
That tug at your hair
Cute bottom for patting
Adorable face
A bundle of joy
To love and embrace
~ Unknown

PRECIOUS LITTLE ONE

Gingham paper: O'Scrap

Lipstick Squared paper: KI Memories

Alphadotz words, Hugz frames: Scrapworks

Simply Stated rub-on transfers: Making Memories

Textured pink paper, vellum, ribbon, and brads from my stash

I'd do it all again...
Our 10ᵗʰ anniversary was so special.
Denny, the hopeless romantic came
through again. After dinner he
asked me to come into the family
room so he could give me my gift.
He gave Tyler the camera to take
shots of the event, and Tyler and
Kyle looked on as he proposed to me
once again, after 10 years. He
dropped down to one knee and
asked me if I had a choice, would I
do it all over again. I very
emphatically responded, "Yes, of
course I would". Then he gave me a
heart shaped diamond pendant.
Every time I wear it I think of
August 1, 1997.

TRUE LOVE

Cardstock: Bazzill Basics

Simply Stated rub-on transfers, Twistel ties:
    Making Memories

Embroidery floss: J. & P. Coats

Embossing powder: PSX

Vellum and buttons from my stash

Font: Lucida Handwriting

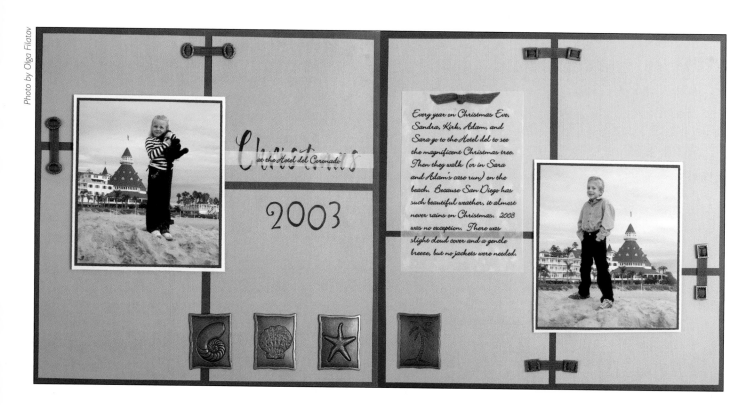

Christmas
at the Hotel del Coronado

2003

Every year on Christmas Eve, Sandra, Kirk, Adam, and Sara go to the Hotel del to see the magnificent Christmas tree. Then they walk (or in Sara and Adam's case run) on the beach. Because San Diego has such beautiful weather, it almost never rains on Christmas. 2003 was no exception. There was slight cloud cover and a gentle breeze, but no jackets were needed.

CHRISTMAS AT THE HOTEL DEL CORONADO

Cardstock: Bazzill Basics

Charmed plaques, ribbon charms: Making Memories

Ribbon: EK Success Adornaments

Font: Bickley Script

Vellum takes longer to dry than regular paper does; be sure not to touch the ink for 2–3 minutes, or it will smear.

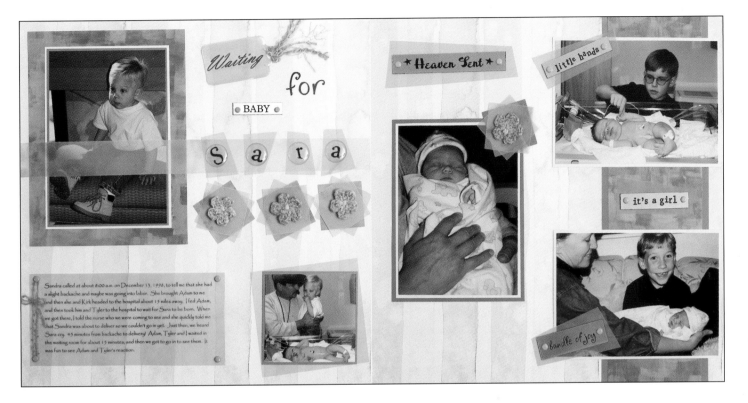

WAITING FOR BABY SARA

Striped paper: Cut It Up

Purple paper and brads from my stash

Bits & Baubles, David Walker Basic ABC, Sonnets Poemstones by Sharon Soneff, square punch: Creative Imaginations

Georgia vellum: The Robin's Nest

Flowers: Dress It Up

Fibers: Making Memories Funky with Fibers

Metallic accents: Die Cuts with a View

Embossing powder: PSX

Fonts: Papyrus, Vladimir Script

tip **When printing on vellum or transparency film, always set your printer to transparency mode to achieve the best results.**

Handmade Paper

I love the beautiful look of handmade papers, especially those with pressed flowers, leaves, and fibers. They make classy journal boxes for outdoor or wedding layouts.

The key to successfully printing on this paper is to make sure that the leading edge (the edge that first feeds into the printer) is cut straight. This allows the printer to pull the paper straight through and will eliminate jamming. Use a 12-inch paper trimmer to cut the leading edge of the paper, and one side if necessary, to ensure that the paper is not wider than the printer can handle. I've had the best luck removing all paper from the paper tray and hand feeding the sheet through the printer by slightly nudging the back edge of the paper.

Handmade paper looks great when you tear the edge of the paper. Be sure to leave enough room around the text to allow for tearing. Some handmade papers are quite thick, and the fibers can make them difficult to tear. If this is the case, use small, flat-edge pliers to grip and tear small sections of the paper from the edges.

 tip **Set your printer driver to plain paper so that the ink won't oversaturate the page.**

GENERATION AFTER GENERATION

Delphinium Solid paper: Colorbök

Handmade straw paper from my stash

Brown mesh: Magic Scraps

Wooden tiles: Making Memories

Wedding alphabet: Paper House Productions

Classic alphabet stickers: Mrs. Grossman's

Metal art: K&Company

Tea-stained tag, stamp ABC, black typewriter, aged typewriter stickers: Sticko Nostalgiques

Font: Vintage Typewriter

There were 13 boys, including Tyler who helped build a hiking trail in Elfin Forest for Stuart McKim's Eagle Project. It was a lot of heavy work selecting and carrying large, rectangular rocks from the rock quarry. They loaded the rocks into a truck, then drove over to the trail, put them on a sled, and hauled them down the trail. The final step was to dig out the dirt and carefully place and secure them. There were some happy hikers that thanked the boys for improving their trail. The burned manzanita and the beautiful flower are evidence of new growth after a devastating wildfire.

STUART'S EAGLE PROJECT

Bijou Verdigris paper: Paper Adventures

Cardstock: Bazzill Basics

Handmade paper from my stash

Dome stickers: K&Company

Fonts: Bodoni MT, Bodoni Black

Cork

Cork is a very interesting medium on which to print titles or journaling. While you can print photos on cork, the dark coloration loses fine details and tends to wash out a photo. However, if you first paint the cork with acrylic paint, your printer will be able to print a photo on it. Cork is a very pliable yet fragile medium. For best results, adhere the cork (on the leading edge and both sides of the paper) to a sheet of cardstock. This will ensure that the paper feeds well through your printer. Printers that load paper from the front and complete a U-turn are not suited to print on cork. Feed the paper/cork through a straight-through path (available on some printers).

Denny truly was born before his time. He is absolutely in his element when he dons his handmade buckskins and beaver hat to go camping and shooting. Had he lived in the 1800's you'd be reading about him in the history books.

100 YEARS TOO LATE

Buckskin paper: The Paper Patch

Hemp fabric and cork from my stash

Distress ink: Ranger Industries

Rectangle zipper pulls: All My Memories

Round stamped alphabet: Life's Journey—K&Company

Font: Book Antiqua

Song of the Old Sewing Machine

Listen up, folks, and I'll tell you my story
About a life of hard work, with touches of glory,
Though confusing at times, there was also great fun
For clothing my family's the best thing I've done.

I stitched and I patched, my treadle it hummed,
With nothing to sew, I'd have truly been bummed!

It started 'way back in the year Nineteen-Eighteen
When a new bride came to buy a sewing machine.
Ida, her name was, and she was lovely to see;
Truly happy was I when she chose to buy me!

So I sewed now and then, but my day wasn't full;
With just two in my family, life seemed a bit dull.

Time went by, and I'll tell you, things changed quite a lot.
Our family grew rapidly, and my needle stayed hot!
I no longer whined and grumbled about nothing to do,
For there were soon six to sew for, instead of just two!

Oh, my treadle whirred and my needle it flashed,
And all hope of finishing was very soon dashed.

The seasons came and they went, and our family it grew;
Would you believe ten by Nineteen Thirty-Two?
Eight children, now, a household both noisy and hectic,
Their clothes had become somewhat worn and eclectic!

I sewed dresses and coats, some small fingers, to boot.
Needle bobbing, treadle speeding, it was truly a hoot!

But I'll enlighten you now, for all hard work aside;
On dull days, with little to do, I became a fun ride!
I had wheels, don't you see; on my lid perched one child,
With two pushing and steering, entertainment was wild!

Down the hall, wheels a'spinning, clickety-clack,
What fun; then a voice: "Put that thing back"!

Then one day, utter silence; oh, what had transpired?
And it came to me, finally, that I'd been retired!
For Ida was gone, there no longer to guide me,
I was lost, floundering, completely at sea!

So I fretted and stewed, consumed in my grief,
When a kind soul claimed me, and now I'm at peace.

Now, here I sit, reminiscing, with nothing to do
But recall those days when, a bit harried, we two
Sat sewing and patching, far into the night.
It was work, I remember, but at times a delight!

And my needle still flashes, my treadle it whirrs,
As I dream of the old days and the love that it stirs.

By Minnehaha
Sewing Machine (Ret.)

SONG OF THE OLD SEWING MACHINE

Nostalgiques baby clothes stickers, epoxy donuts: EK Success

Button paper: K&Company

Linen paper: Bo-Bunny Press

EZ Walnut Ink TintZ: Fiber Scraps

Ribbon: Making Memories

Poem written by Betty Parsell

Cork, vellum, burlap, yarn, fibers, and buttons from my stash

Font: Times New Roman

Cardstock and Printed Papers

Cardstock is another great type of paper for printing photos and text. The linen-textured paper makes a beautiful photo with a muted look to it. These photos work really well for backgrounds when a more prominent true photo is in the foreground, or even as a background for a full page of journaling. It's also fun to print on preprinted paper. A subtle pattern can enhance a photo by gently peeking through the image.

Enhance your cardstock journaling or photo by using decorative chalks. You can color the edge of the photo or journal, use chalk to highlight special words, or fill in highlights on a black-and-white photo.

THE TREE

Pine tree paper: Paper Adventures

Alphabet charms: Making Memories

Tree from my stash

Red stitch frame: Heidi Grace

Checked paper: Creative Memories

Metallic thread: Kreinik

David Walker ABC stickers: Creative Imaginations

Curly alphabet stickers: Me & My Big Ideas

Decorative chalk: Craf-T Products

CK Journaling font: Creating Keepsakes

HANDMADE WITH LOVE

Cardstock: Bazzill Basics

Beaded star paper from my stash

Alphabet charms: Making Memories

Font: Angelina

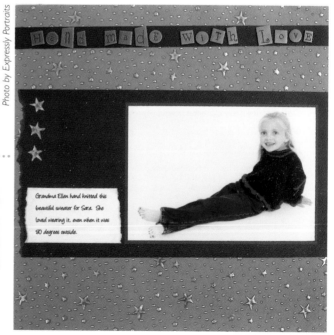

Photo by Expressly Portraits

OUR NEW WHEELS

Cardstock: Bazzill Basics

Blue glossy paper: NRN Designs

Denim stripe paper: Bo-Bunny Press

Blue splatter paper: Making Memories

Stamps: Hero Arts

Crystal Pigment ink pad: Rubber Stampede

Font: Tempus Sans ITC

Buttons from my stash

Tyler and Kyle were so excited to get new car beds. They couldn't wait until Dad put them together. Kyle put the bed to the "jumping" test and it passed with flying colors.   April 1994

PUPPY LOVE

Cardstock: Bazzill Basics

Green speckled paper, blue speckled paper, fibers: Making Memories

Life's Journey stickers: K&Company

Mesh: Maruyama Magenta

Square punch: Creative Memories

Walnut ink: Tsukineko

Fibers: EK Success Adornaments

Bits and baubles: Creative Imaginations

Nostalgiques alphabet stickers: Rebecca Sower

Eyelets: JewelCraft

Brown fiber scraps and brads from my stash

Font: Tempus Sans ITC

Kyle had been begging us for a new puppy for about six months. We already had one dog and several cats, so we really didn't want another pet. We finally decided to buy him an electronic puppy named Gigi, which barked, walked, and jumped. He was thrilled, and there were no puppy messes to clean up.

Tyler

You were so excited to
be a ring bearer in
Aunt Mary's wedding.
You did your job well
and we were so proud
of you.

1/6/96

TYLER

Cardstock: Bazzill Basics

Soft velvet sheer paper: Maruyama Magenta

Grape Odyssey paper: Memories Magenta Style

Maggie tags and papers: Dolphin Enterprises

Metallic paper: The Paper Co.

Details corners, oval frame: Making Memories

Rings: Modern Romance

Decorating chalk: Craf-T Products

Vellum, ribbon from my stash

Font: Fine Hand

Mulberry Paper

Mulberry paper is a very thin and fragile paper that can be used to add a soft or sheer look to your page. I used it to tone down the bold colors of playing cards by layering the mulberry paper on top of the cards in the Discover layout.

You can print on mulberry paper despite its fragility; following these guidelines will lead you to success.

Do not try to feed a sheet of mulberry paper into your printer without adhering it to a sheet of plain paper. The mulberry paper will crumple and could jam—if not seriously damage—your printer. Apply a temporary adhesive such as Hermafix along the leading edge (the edge that feeds first into the printer) and both vertical edges of a piece of plain paper. Carefully adhere the mulberry paper to the plain paper and rub the edge several times to be sure the mulberry paper sticks.

Remove all other paper from the paper tray and hand feed the adhered sheets into the printer. If you are unsure as to which side of the paper to place up in the paper tray, refer to your printer documentation.

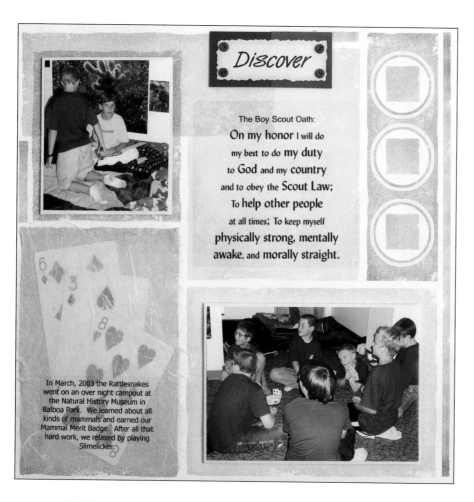

 Set your print quality to normal/draft to apply the least amount of ink and avoid bleeding.

DISCOVER

Paper: Carolee's Creations

Scout embellishments: It Takes Two

Fibers: EK Success Adornaments

Discover tag: Paper Bliss

Mulberry paper and playing cards from my stash

Transparency film

Font: Tahoma

HEAT
embossing

Heat embossing is a fun and easy way to add dimension to your flat, printed photo or text. You have to work fast, though, as the ink from your printer can dry quite rapidly. Heat embossing works best on vellum, transparency film, and embossing inkjet papers, as they tend to dry more slowly because the ink sits on the surface and does not absorb into the medium.

Experiment with different colors of embossing powder. Clear powder enhances and brightens the colors. Pearlescent gives more of an elegant muted look and really goes well with shabby chic and nostalgic designs. Silver or gold is an excellent powder to use for titles and for journaling on formal pages, but use it sparingly as it can tend to become heavy and thick.

You can emboss your photos as well for a very unique look. Emboss a photo taken in the rain or of your dog playing in the sprinklers. Embossing makes the photo come alive!

Design a page in your word processor, graphics, font, or journaling program. Place a scrap piece of paper on your work surface to catch any residual powder. As soon as the scrapbook page has printed, sprinkle embossing powder on the wet ink. Tap the excess off onto the scrap piece of paper. The embossing powder will adhere to the ink. Immediately use your heat gun to melt and set the powder.

1. Place a sheet of scrap paper on your work surface to catch the excess embossing powder. Print your text or photo on a piece of vellum or inkjet transparency film.

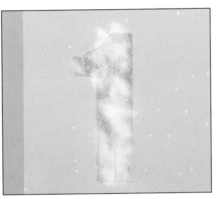

2. Immediately remove the printed piece from the printer and lightly dust the ink with embossing powder.

3. Carefully curl the edges of the printed sheet and tap it several times on the paper on your work surface to remove excess powder.

If there is extra powder clinging to a nonprinted area, use a fine, dry paintbrush to gently brush it away.

4. Use your heat gun (not a hair dryer) to melt the embossing powder. As the powder melts, the ink goes from being dull to vibrant.

5. Roll your scrap paper with the excess powder into a cone and tap the remaining powder back into the container. Embossing powder goes a long way.

bubbles

Even at 15, Tyler and Sean are not too old for bubbles. They had a contest to see who could make the biggest one. Sean's was big, but Tyler's was HUGE!

BUBBLES

Sprinkles light blue paper: All My Memories

Buttons: Sticko by Stickopotamus

Stickers: Me & My Big Ideas, Stickopotamus

Sonnets Poemstones by Sharon Soneff: Creative Imaginations

 tip Set your printer driver to transparency when printing on vellum or transparency film. This will put less ink on the page and slow down the print speed so the ink doesn't smear.

OH, THE LAUGH OF A CHILD

Cardstock: Bazzill Basics

Little Boy Blue splatter paper, Simple Sayings sticker: Bo-Bunny Press

Wordz, Sonnets Poemstones by Sharon Soneff: Creative Imaginations

Details frames, brads: Making Memories

Fibers: EK Success Adornments, Making Memories Funky with Fibers

Vellum: American Crafts

Mesh: Magic Mesh

Brads: JewelCraft

Embossing powder: PSX

Transparency film

Font: Bradley Hand ITC

 The embossing gun/tool gets very hot. Hold your paper by one corner and heat the area furthest away from your hand. Do not set the paper on carpet or linoleum, as the heat can melt these surfaces.

Oh the laugh of a child
so wild and so free
Is the merriest sound
in the world to me

our
HAPPY
silly
energetic
SWEET
Special
precious
BOY

smile

Kyle, April 1994

 Fine or extra-fine powder will enhance any fine details.

I hope you'll find these new techniques full of inspiration to help you make your most creative layouts ever! Although some of the techniques shown will stretch the capabilities of your printer, I want to assure you that no printer was harmed during any of these projects.

Printing photos, journaling and embellishments is as easy as turning on your computer. Practice these techniques and your printer will soon become one of your favorite scrapbooking tools.

FOR MORE INFORMATION, ASK FOR A FREE CATALOG:

C&T Publishing, Inc.

P.O. Box 1456

Lafayette, CA 94549

(800) 284-1114

ctinfo@ctpub.com

www.ctpub.com

FOR FABRICS AND SEWING SUPPLIES:

Cotton Patch Mail Order

3405 Hall Lane, Dept. CTB

Lafayette, CA 94549

(800) 835-4418

(925) 283-7883

quiltusa@yahoo.com

www.quiltusa.com

Note: Materials shown on pages may not be currently available as manufacturers keep many items in stock for only a short time.

About the Author

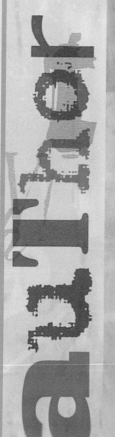

Sue Martin has been scrapbooking for over ten years and crafting her entire life. An accomplished technology guru, she embraces technology and loves to incorporate digital techniques with traditional scrapbooking. She loves to share her experiences and ideas with all who are anxious to learn. She has worked for Hewlett-Packard since 1977 and has been able to influence the design of photo printers, inks, and digital cameras to accommodate the cutting-edge needs of scrapbookers and crafters. Sue has taught technology and scrapbooking classes both in the United States and abroad, in countries such as Greece, the United Kingdom, and Canada. When she's not designing new techniques and layouts, she is very busy with Boy Scouts, designing interiors for custom homes for the family business, and enjoying life with her wonderful husband, Denny, and awesome teenage sons, Tyler and Kyle.

Sources

Some of these companies only sell wholesale, but most websites list where to buy the products retail.

Adobe Systems, Inc. *(Photoshop Elements, Photoshop Pro)*
345 Park Avenue
San Jose, CA 95110
408.536.6000
www.adobe.com

All My Memories *(paper, die cuts, embellishments)*
12218 S. Lone Peak Parkway, Suite 101
Draper, UT 84062
888.553.1998
www.allmymemories.com

American Crafts *(paper, vellum, pens and markers, embellishments)*
476 North 1500 West
Orem, UT 84057
801.226.0747
www.americancrafts.com

ArcSoft Panorama Maker *(computer program)*
46601 Fremont Boulevard
Fremont, CA 94538
510.440.9901
www.arcsoft.com

Artistic Wire *(wire for embellishing)*
752 N. Larch Avenue
Elmhurst, IL 60126
630.530.7567
www.artisticwire.com

Autumn Leaves *(paper, embellishments)*
14140 Ventura Blvd. #202
Sherman Oaks, CA 91423
800.588.6707
www.autumnleaves.com

BasicGrey *(paper)*
1343 Flint Meadow Drive #6
Kaysville, UT 84037
801.544.1116
www.basicgrey.com

Bazzill Basics Paper *(paper, embellishments)*
701 N. Golden Key Street
Gilbert, AZ 85233
480.558.8557
www.bazzillbasics.com

Bo-Bunny Press *(paper, stickers, die cuts)*
2985 North 935 East #9
Layton, UT 84041
801.771.4010
www.bobunny.com

The Card Connection *(embellishments)*
Found exclusively at Michaels stores
800.873.5506

Coats & Clark *(J.P. & Coats embroidery floss)*
P.O. Box 12229
Greenville, SC 29612-0229
800.648.1479
www.coatsandclark.com

Carolace *(lace embellishments)*
65 Railroad Avenue, Unit #3
Ridgefield, NJ 07657
201.945.2151
www.carolace.com

Carolee's Creations *(paper, embellishments)*
3339 N. US Highway 91
Hyde Park, UT 84318
435.563.1100
www.caroleescreations.com

Cloud 9 Design *(paper, stickers, embellishments)*
8710 Jefferson Highway
Osseo, MN 55369
763.493.0990
www.cloud9design.biz

Colorbök *(paper, die-cut frames)*
2716 Baker Road
Dexter, MI 48130
www.colorbok.com

Creating Keepsakes Magazine *(fonts and clip art)*
14850 Pony Express Road
Bluffdale, UT 84065
801.984.2070
www.creatingkeepsakes.com

Creative Imaginations *(Scrapper's Canvas and more)*
17832 Gothard Street
Huntington Beach, CA 92647
800.942.6487
www.cigift.com

Creative Impressions *(cork paper, twill tape, stamps, embellishments)*
1205 Shasta Drive
Colorado Springs, CO 80910
719.596.4860
www.creativeimpressions.com

Creative Memories *(paper and embellishments)*
P.O. Box 1839
St. Cloud, MN 56302
800.468.9335
www.creative-memories.com

Cut It Up *(paper, inks, paints, embellishments)*
P.O. Box 287
Gold Run, CA 95717
530.389.2233
www.cut-it-up.com

Daisy D's *(paper)*
375 West 200 South, Suite 200
Salt Lake City, UT 84101
888.601.8955
www.daisydspaper.com

Déjà Views *(vellum words and phrases, and more)*
The C-Thru Ruler Co.
6 Britton Drive
Bloomfield CT 06002
800.243.8419
www.dejaviews.com/deja/

Delta Technical Coatings *(paint)*
2550 Pellissier Place
Whittier, CA 90601
800.423.4135
www.deltacrafts.com

Die Cuts with a View *(die cuts and metal accents)*
2250 N. University Parkway #486
Provo, UT 84604
801.224.6766
www.diecutswithaview.com

Dolphin Enterprises *(paper, tags, and more)*
5180 South 300 West, Suite E
Salt Lake City, UT 84107
877.910.3306
www.protect-a-page.com

Doodlebug Design *(paper, embellishments)*
2181 W. California Avenue, Suite 100
Salt Lake City, UT 84104
801.952.0555
www.doodlebug.ws

Dress It Up *(buttons, beads, tags)*
P.O. Box 1248
Berlin, MD 21811
888.811.7441
www.dressitupbuttonsandtrim.com

EK Success *(vellum, embellishments, Hermafix, Stickopotamus, and more)*
P.O. Box 1141
Clifton, NJ 07014
800.524.1349
www.eksuccess.com

Fiber Scraps *(fiber embellishments)*
82 Windover Lane
Doylestown, PA 18901
215.230.4905
www.fiberscraps.com

Fredrix *(Tygerag)*
P.O. Box 646
Lawrenceville, GA 30046
www.fredrixartistcanvas.com

Heidi Grace Designs *(paper, embellishments, transfers)*
301 W. Main Street
Auburn, WA 98001
866.894.3434
www.heidigrace.com

Hero Arts *(rubber stamps, paper, accessories)*
1343 Powell Street
Emeryville, CA 94608
800.822.4376
www.heroarts.com

Hewlett-Packard Company *(photo paper, Creative Scrapbook Assistant software, printers, cameras)*
3000 Hanover Street
Palo Alto, CA 94304
888.999.4747
www.shopping.hp.com

Hirschberg Schutz & Co., Inc. *(embellishments)*
Found at Michaels stores
800.873.5506

It Takes Two *(paper, embellishments)*
100 Minnesota Avenue
Le Sueur, MN 56058
800.331.9483
www.ittakestwo.com

JewelCraft *(beads, embellishments)*
505 Winsor Drive
Secaucus, NJ 07094
201.223.0804
www.jewelcraft.biz

June Tailor *(printable fabric, thread, accessories)*
2861 Highway 175
Richfield, WI 53076
800.844.5400
www.junetailor.com

Junkitz *(embellishments)*
17 Sweetmans Lane, Building 12
Manalpan, NJ 07726
732.792.1108
www.junkitz.com

K&Company *(paper, stickers, embellishments)*
8500 N.W. River Park Drive, Pillar #136
Parkville, MO 64152
816.389.4150
www.kandcompany.com

Karen Foster Design *(paper, embellishments)*
623 North 1250 West
Centerville, UT 84014
801.451.9779
www.karenfosterdesign.com

KI Memories *(paper, embellishments)*
3720 Arapaho Road
Addison, TX 75001
972.243.5595
www.kimemories.com

Kreinik Mfg. Co., Inc. *(thread, embellishments)*
3106 Lord Baltimore Drive, Suite 101
Baltimore, MD 21244
410.281.0040
www.kreinik.com

Li'l Davis Designs *(embellishments)*
17835 Sky Park Circle, Suite D
Irvine, CA 92164
949.838.0344
www.lildavisdesigns.com

Lion Brand Yarn *(yarn, fibers)*
135 Kero Road
Carlstadt, NJ 07072
800.258.9276
www.lionbrand.com

Magic Mesh *(Magic Mesh)*
P.O. Box 8
Lake City, MN 55041
651.345.6374
www.magicmesh.com

Magic Scraps *(shaker boxes, embellishments, and more)*
1232 Exchange Drive
Richardson, TX 75081
972.238.1838
www.magicscraps.com

Making Memories *(paper, embellishments, and more)*
1168 West 500 North
Centerville, UT 84014
801.294.0430
www.makingmemories.com

Maruyama Magenta *(paper, mesh, embellishments)*
2275 Bombardier
Sainte-Julie, QC J3E 2J9
Canada
450.922.5253
www.magentastyle.com

Me & My Big Ideas *(paper, embellishments)*
20321 Valencia Circle
Lake Forest, CA 92630
949.583.2065
www.meandmybigideas.com

Memories Complete *(paper, vellum, stickers, embellishments, and more)*
329 South 860 East #5
American Fork, UT 84003
866.966.6365
www.memoriescomplete.com

Memory Bound *(paper)*
641 N. Ankeny Boulevard
Ankeny, IA 50021
515.577.6698
www.memoryboundproducts.com

Michaels Stores, Inc. *(paper, tools, embellishments, and more)*
8000 Bent Branch Drive
Irving, TX 75063
800.642.4235
www.michaels.com

Micro Format, Inc. *(paper, embossing powder, and more)*
830–3 Seton Court
Wheeling, IL 60090
800.333.0549
www.paper-paper.com

Microsoft Corporation *(WordArt, Microsoft Word)*
1 Microsoft Way
Redmond, WA 98052
800.642.7676
www.microsoft.com

Mrs. Grossman's *(stickers, paper)*
P.O. Box 4467
Petaluma, CA 94955
800.429.4549
www.mrsgrossmans.com

Mustard Moon *(paper, stickers)*
www.mustardmoon.com

NRN Designs *(paper)*
5142 Argosy Avenue
Huntington Beach, CA 92649
800.421-6958
www.nrndesigns.com

O'Scrap *(paper, embellishments, and more)*
P.O. Box 307
Orem, UT 84059
801.225.6015
www.oscrap.com

Paper Adventures *(paper, embellishments, and more)*
901 S. 5th Street
Milwaukee, WI 53204
414.645.5760
www.paperadventures.com

Paper Bliss *(paper, die cuts, tools, embellishments)*
Westrim Crafts
7855 Havenhurst Avenue
Van Nuys, CA 91406
800.727.2727
www.westrimcrafts.com

The Paper Co. *(paper)*
510 Ryerson Road
Lincoln Park, NJ 07035
973.406.5000

Paper House Productions *(paper, stickers, die cuts)*
1760 Glasco Turnpike
Woodstock, NY 12498
800.255.7316
www.paperhouseproductions.com

The Paper Patch *(paper, stickers)*
P.O. Box 217
West Jordan, UT 84088
www.paperpatch.com

The Paper Loft *(paper)*
P.O. Box 95407
South Jordan, UT 84095
801.254.1961
www.paperloft.com

Paper Wishes *(Paper Pizazz line)*
1250 NW Third
Canby, OR 97013
888.300.3406
www.paperwishes.com

Plaid *(paints)*
P.O. Box 7600
Norcross, GA 30091
800.842.4197
www.plaidonline.com

Pressed Petals *(embellishments)*
47 S. Main Street
Richfield, UT 84701
800.748.4656
www.pressedpetals.com

Provo Craft *(paper)*
151 East 3450 North
Spanish Fork, UT 84660
800.937.7686
www.provocraft.com

PSX *(embossing powder)*
Duncan Enterprises
5673 E. Shields Avenue
Fresno, CA 93727
800.438.6226
www.psxdesign.com

Queen & Company *(brads)*
P.O. Box 501773
San Diego, CA 92150
858.613.7858
www.queenandcompany.com

Ranger Industries *(inks, stamp cleaners, and more)*
15 Park Road
Tinton Falls, NJ 07724
732.389.3535
www.rangerink.com

The Robin's Nest *(paper, vellum)*
1179 North 3000 West
Vernal, UT 84078
435.789.5387

Rubber Stampede *(stamps, paints, inks, FabriCraft)*
2550 Pellissier Place
Whittier, CA 90601
800.423.4135
www.rubberstampede.com

Sandylion Sticker Designs *(stickers)*
P.O. Box 1570
Buffalo, NY 14240
800.387.4215
www.sandylion.com

Scrapbook Sally *(paper, vellum, embellishments)*
1920 28th Street N.E.
Calgary, Alberta T2A-6K1
Canada
866.SB.SALLY
www.scrapbooksally.com

Scrap-ease *(embellishments)*
3449 East Kael Street
Mesa, AZ 85213
480.830.4581
www.scrap-ease.com

Scrapworks *(embellishments)*
3038 Specialty Circle, Suite C
Salt Lake City, UT 84115
801.363.1010
www.scrapworks.com

S.E.I. *(paper)*
1717 South 450 West
Logan, UT 84321
800.333.3279
www.shopsei.com

Stampendous *(rubber stamps)*
1240 N. Red Gum Street
Anaheim, CA 92806
800.869.0474
www.stampendous.com

Staples *(transparency film, office supplies)*
500 Staples Drive
Framingham, MA 01702
800.3STAPLE (800.378.2753)
www.staples.com

Suze Weinberg Designs *(embellishments, tools)*
1301 West Park Avenue
Ocean, NJ 07712
732.493.1390
www.schmoozewithsuze.com

Tsukineko *(Versamark inks, ink pads)*
17640 N.E. 65th Street
Redmond, WA 98052
425.883.7733
www.tsukineko.com

Wrights *(rickrack, ribbon, braid, chains)*
P.O. Box 398
West Warren, MA 01092
877.597.4448
www.wrights.com